OCEANS

KINGFISHER

KINGFISHER

First published 2012 by Kingfisher
an imprint of Macmillan Children's Books
a division of Macmillan Publishers Limited
20 New Wharf Road, London N1 9RR
Basingstoke and Oxford
Associated companies throughout the world
www.panmacmillan.com

ISBN 978-0-7534-3344-7

Consultant: Dr Frances Dipper

Designed and created by Basher www.basherbooks.com
Text written by Dan Green

Dedicated to Dave (master chicken), Ness and Leela

Text and design copyright © Toucan Books Ltd 2012
Based on an original concept by Toucan Books Ltd
Illustrations copyright © Simon Basher 2012

9 8 7 6 5 4 3 2 1
1TR/1111/WKT/UNTD/140MA

A CIP catalogue record for this book
is available from the British Library.

Printed in China

Note to readers: the website addresses listed above are correct at
the time of going to print. However, due to the ever-changing nature
of the internet, website addresses and content can change. Websites
can contain links that are unsuitable for children. The publisher cannot
be held responsible for changes in website addresses or content, or for
information obtained through a third party. We strongly advise that
internet searches should be supervised by an adult.

CONTENTS

Introduction

Oceans

Welcome to the Big Blue – an endless expanse of water that covers most of planet Earth. A million mysteries lurk within these murky depths: creatures living here have to prevent salt drying out their bodies; there's only light for the first 100–200 m; temperatures plummet beneath the waves; pressure rises with depth; and sound travels great distances. You've got it – this is one weird, watery realm.

The most recent tally of all ocean life counted 230,000 species, with at least four times that still awaiting discovery. Your guide to this alien environment is Captain Jacques Cousteau (1910–1997). This Frenchman was an eccentric and a pioneering explorer, scientist, filmmaker, author and co-inventor of the aqualung (phew!). He made 120 TV documentaries and wrote more than 50 books – his work revealed the hidden underwater world. Jacques was one of the first to think about how humans can harm ocean life and what we can do to protect this eyeball-achingly amazing environment. The ocean is so vast, this book can only dip a toe beneath the surface, but what are you waiting for? Come on in, the water's lovely!

Jacques Cousteau

Chapter 1
Water World

Our planet is very special indeed. It's the only one in the entire Solar System that has liquid water on its surface. In fact, almost three-quarters of this mighty orb is covered in oceans and seas. It makes you wonder who decided to call it "Earth" in the first place, since any Noddy can see that it's mainly water! So take this rare opportunity to meet the wet, wild Water World crew. You'll encounter mountains higher than anything on dry land, trenches deeper than Mount Everest is high and mind-blowingly huge plains. And let's not forget the salt-stained captain of them all – Ocean! Just wade this way...

Ocean

Seas

Zones

Mid-ocean Ridge

Trench

Ocean
Water World

- This salty fellow covers 66 per cent of the Earth's surface
- Makes up almost three-quarters of the planet's hydrosphere
- The hydrosphere is all water in, on and around the planet

I am the blue-eyed giant, reaching far and wide across the planet's surface. Gaze into my depths and you'll see wonders and mysteries that will blow your mind!

My great volume acts as a sink for the Sun's energy. I soak up its rays, helping to keep Earth warm and affecting its climate. My currents drive the globe's wind patterns. Though I have just one body, I am subdivided into five mammoth oceans. The biggest is Pacific, which stretches majestically between the Americas, Asia and Australia. Atlantic – the saltiest ocean – reaches from Europe to the Americas. Warm Indian Ocean hugs the east coast of Africa up to India, while frigid Southern Ocean wraps around Antarctica. Lastly, small, frozen-over Arctic Ocean sits all a-shiver at the North Pole. Brrr!

- Area of all oceans: 360 million km²
- Volume of all oceans: approximately 1.3 billion km³
- Average depth of the oceans: 3790 m

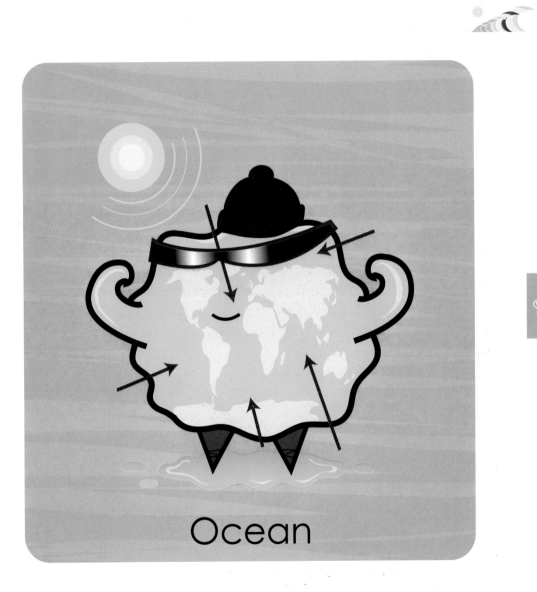

Ocean

9

Seas
■ Water World

- ✳ Large areas of salt water connected to the ocean
- ✳ Can be cut off from the ocean completely (e.g. Caspian Sea)
- ✳ These bodies include gulfs, inlets, passages and bays

Ahoy there! We are Ocean's little friends. Our boots may be smaller and take less to fill, but we're an important part of Earth's fascinating saltwater story.

The difference between us and Ocean is that we are often surrounded by land (although almost always with a channel to our expansive pal). Our names suggest adventure and romance. Take Celebes, in the western Pacific, with its stunning coral reefs and notorious pirates, or North Atlantic Sargasso – the only sea with no land coasts. Surrounded on all sides by swift Atlantic currents, Sargasso's water is calm, deep blue and crystal clear. Migrating eels journey here to lay their eggs far below the abundant floating seaweed that also shelters young turtles from predators on the prowl.

- ● Largest sea: Philippine Sea (surface area: 5,177,762 km^2)
- ● Amount of salt in 1 litre of seawater: 35 g
- ● Proportion of Earth's biomass in the oceans: over 90 %

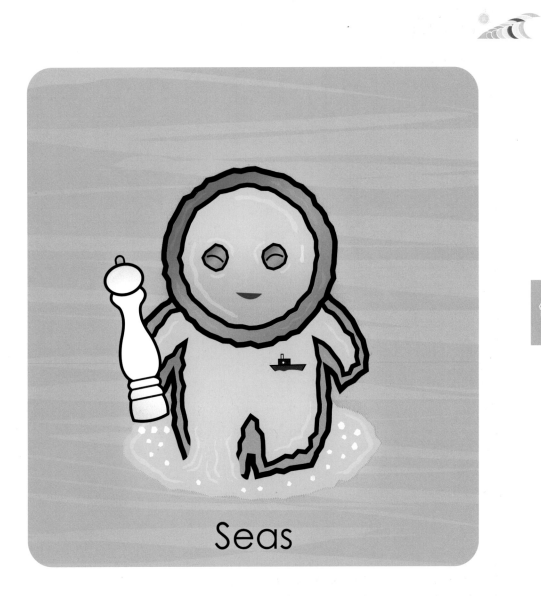

Seas

Zones
■ Water World

✳ Marine environments found at different depths in the ocean
✳ Light, water temperature and water pressure vary per zone
✳ Some form of life can be found in each of the zones

As well as covering area, Ocean also has depth, and that's where we come in. From surface to floor, we change in character the lower we go.

At the top is the sunlit zone. Sufficient light to allow plants to thrive penetrates about 100–150 m, which means that 90 per cent of all ocean life either resides or feeds here. Below this, the twilight zone has the merest hint of blue light. It's extremely cold and the water pressure is crushing. No plants live here, just hungry carnivores. Lower still, the midnight zone stretches to the near-freezing muddy plains of the ocean floor, home to bottom feeders and witching-hour predators. Finally, there's the impressively deep abyssal zone (up to 6000 m) and the hadal zone, where Trench plunges way down, as low as you can go.

● Sunlit zone (a.k.a. epipelagic zone): 0–200 m
● Twilight zone (a.k.a. mesopelagic zone): 200–1000 m
● Midnight zone (a.k.a. bathypelagic zone): 1000–4000 m

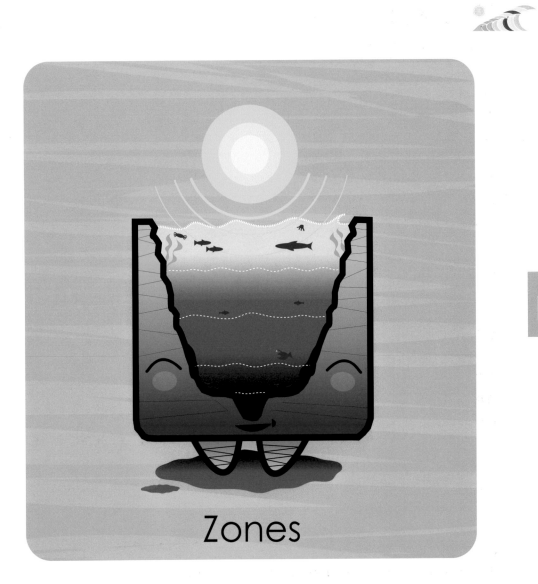

Zones

Mid-ocean Ridge

■ Water World

- ☀ A chain of young mountains that form new ocean floor
- ☀ Longest-known mountain range in the Universe
- ☀ Tall peaks (seamounts) can grow to form mid-ocean islands

Tall and broad of shoulder, I have underwater peaks that dwarf those on land. Seamounts rear up from my ridges, sometimes breaking the surface to form islands and reefs. My ranges are connected to each other and I have a very unique skill. Hot and volcanic, I pump out lava to make new ocean crust as part of a process that slowly pushes the continents apart.

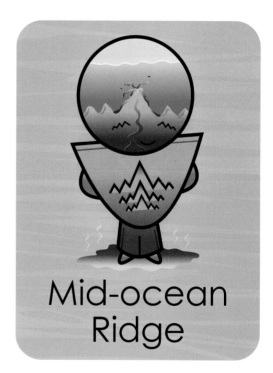

Mid-ocean Ridge

- ● Total length of mid-ocean ridge mountain chains: over 65,000 km
- ● Thickness of ocean crust: 1 to 2 km
- ● Tallest mountain: Mauna Kea, Hawaii (10,203 m from ocean floor to summit)

Trench
Water World ■

- ☀ Deepest, darkest and coldest part of the ocean
- ☀ Great ditches where ocean crust is dragged back into Earth
- ☀ Only three submersibles have ever been this deep

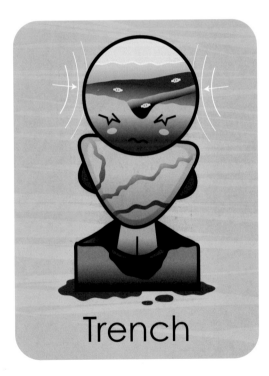

Trench

I am the lowest of the low, a ditch marking where Earth has dragged the ocean floor down into its hungry interior. My deep gullies and fissures plunge suddenly and steeply, thousands of metres below the ocean floor. With head-crushing pressures and water temperatures barely above freezing, humans know more about the surface of the Moon than they do about me.

- ● Ocean's deepest point: 10,924 m (Challenger Deep, Mariana Trench)
- ● Height of Mount Everest: 8848 m
- ● Proper name for the trench zone: hadal zone

Chapter 2
Ocean Motion

With most of the planet covered in slippy-slidey water, this is a world in motion. Wave transports energy across the oceans, as seawater is pushed hither and thither by the wind. It is here that you'll find Tidal Current trying out a few turbulent tricks. Meanwhile, the Moon pulls Earth's surface towards it, creating two bulges as it orbits, and these force moonstruck Tide to rise and fall. Of course, the big player in this great game is Ocean Current. In shifting warm water around the planet, this stirrer and mixer of vast water masses also drives the world's Weather Systems. What a com-"motion"!

Wave

Tide

Tidal Current

Ocean Current

Weather Systems

Wave

Ocean Motion

- An energy surge that travels through water
- Wind-generated waves batter coastlines relentlessly
- Tsunamis are killer waves that are not generated by wind

I'm the lion of the seas. Shaking my mane and roaring out loud, I come crashing down on beaches and cliffs around the world. Life for me is full of ups and downs, but on the whole, I'd say it was pretty *swell*!

Most of the time I am created by the wind. The friction of air against the sea's surface transfers energy from the wind to the water, and starts making the surface bob up and down. I move as a pulse *through* the water rather than taking any of it with me... until I hit the shore, that is. Surfers ride my "breakers" – totally bodacious! Tsunamis are my most terrifying form. Generated by underwater earthquakes, landslides, explosions or falling meteorites, these monster waves travel huge distances, almost invisibly, wreaking destruction wherever they hit land.

- Highest-ever measured storm wave: 29.1 m (as tall as a ten-storey building)
- Biggest tsunami wave: 520 m (Lituya Bay, Alaska, 1958)
- A rubber duck moves in circular loops on a wave, with little forward motion

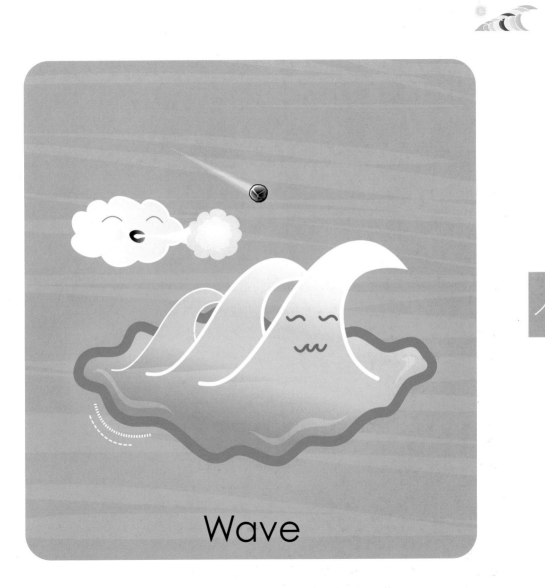

Wave

Tide

■ Ocean Motion

✳ This in-and-out fella's having a love affair with the Moon
✳ Lunar gravitation attraction causes sea levels to rise and fall
✳ Most places have two high tides and two low tides each day

I'm a bit of a lunatic! As the Moon passes overhead, the water in the ocean feels a tug towards it. That's gravity. In fact, the whole planet feels this force of attraction, but since water is freer to move than land, it is pulled this way and that, and so sloshes about the planet a bit.

At high tide, the water level at the coast rises. Harbours and estuaries fill, waves break closer to shore and tidal surges, called bores, race up river channels against the normal direction of flow. At low tide, harbours and estuaries empty, waves break further out, mudflats are exposed, rock pools form and seashore life is left shivering in the Sun. Spring tides happen whenever the Sun and Moon line up. The extra pull that this creates means the tides are exceptionally high. That's that *tide* up, I think.

● Biggest recorded tidal range: 21.6 m (Bay of Fundy, Canada)
● Spring tide: approx. 20 % higher than normal
● Neap tide (alternates with spring tide): approx. 20 % lower than normal

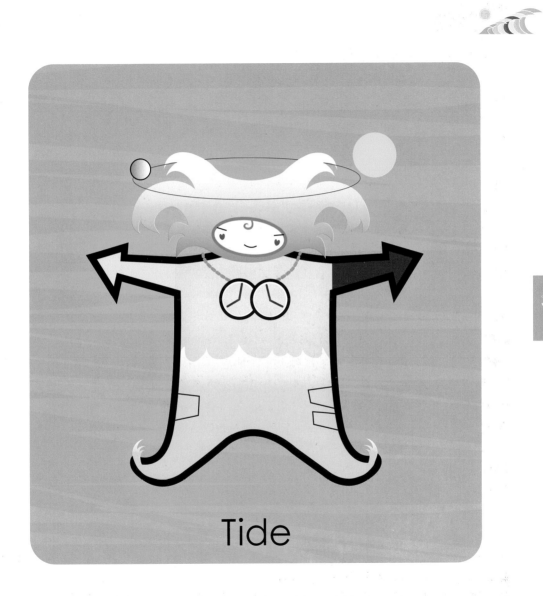

Tide

Tidal Current
Ocean Motion

☀ Strong rush or race of water at, or just below, the surface
☀ Its backdrafts, swirls and eddies make swimming dangerous
☀ Often occurs at beaches when the tide turns

I am a devious trickster and thoroughly dangerous to know. I've got a bunch of nasty pranks up my sleeve and I'm *currently* working out a way to drag you down.

I've got a mind of my own, often rushing in channels of swift-flowing water. I love to go against the flow. Undertow is the drag-back of a wave, powerful enough to knock you off your feet. A riptide is a surface race, caused when water is pushed sideways along the shore by more waves breaking behind it. This water rushes back to sea through channels, flattening the incoming waves. It makes the sea look calm, but really it's deadly, and can whisk you away from safety. My meanest form is the maelstrom, a wild whirlpool that can suck objects deeper than 100 m below the waves and pull them along the sea floor.

● World's strongest whirlpool: Saltstraumen (Norway)
● Skookumchuck: a powerful tidal rapid at a river mouth
● On average, riptides are more deadly than lightning, hurricanes and tornadoes

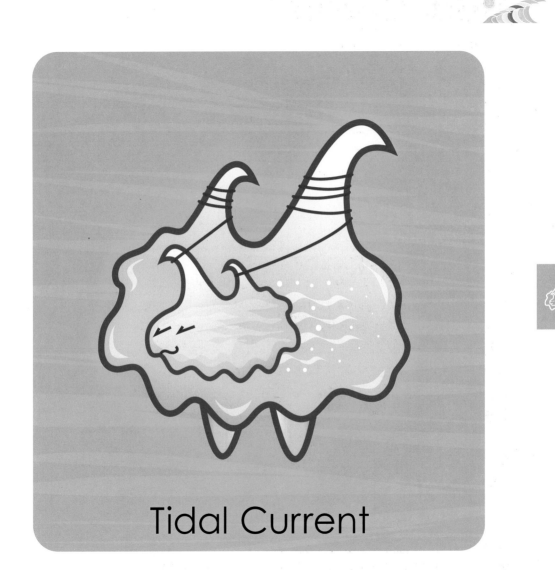

Tidal Current

Ocean Current
Ocean Motion

* Large-scale movement of great masses of ocean water
* Called a gyre, there are five of these mammoths in total
* These vast water loops are driven by the planet's rotation

Wimpy Tidal Current is little more than a stirrer compared to me. When it comes to moving water about, I send it around the world! You got it baby, I'm a prime mixer.

With names like North Atlantic Ocean Gyre and Indian Ocean Gyre, I may sound a little dull, but don't you believe it. Driven by Earth's spin, I swirl around in huge, closed loops, speeding ships on their way. Meanwhile, my deeper self gets busy swirling seawater below the surface. Differences in temperature and density drive deepwater currents that bring warmth to polar seas (think Gulf Stream). When these deep waters surface, they bring nutrients up from the depths, and provide rich feeding grounds for sealife. These creatures use my swift submarine expressways to travel the oceans speedily.

● Unit of measurement: Sverdrup (Sv); 1 Sv=1,000,000 m^3 seawater per second
● Largest ocean current: Antarctic Circumpolar Current (125 Sv)
● Global Ocean Conveyor Belt: another name for deepwater currents

Ocean Current

Weather Systems
Ocean Motion

- ✳ Movers and shakers that help to regulate the global climate
- ✳ Aid the shifting of warm water around the planet
- ✳ Trade winds carry dust from Africa as far as the Caribbean

Ocean Current and I are coupled together like a car and trailer, but sometimes it's hard to know who's doing the pushing and who's pulling!

At the Equator, trade winds blow westwards, set in motion by the warming Sun and deflected by Earth's rotation. These winds move ocean water about, and together they create my climate patterns, which affect whole regions of the planet. But I'm also driven by Ocean Current: for example, the flow of warm water northwards from the tropics is one of the reasons why the North Pole is warmer than the South Pole. Elsewhere, a rise in temperature of the surface waters in the Pacific Ocean creates El Niño episodes about every five years – effectively a reversal of the normal weather cycle.

- ● Monsoon rain: up to 10,000 mm (Indian subcontinent: June to September)
- ● Average duration of a cyclone: 1 week
- ● El Niña: the counterpart to El Niño, bringing lower than normal sea temperatures

Weather Systems

Chapter 3
Shoreline Gang

The shallow-water zones surrounding Earth's landmasses are a mere drop in the ocean's total volume, but they supply more than 90 per cent of our seafood. Young fish stay here until they're big enough to venture out into open water. Closer in, the shore is licked by waves and washed by tides to create a range of different habitats – from sandy beaches, rocky shores and cliffs, to vast mudflats and mangroves. This place is teeming with creatures who are submerged one moment and stranded without water the next. Take a look in any rock pool and you'll find a very special crew scuttling away from you!

Seaweed

Seashells

Sea Slug

Sea Anemone

Sea Urchin

Prawn

Barnacle

Crab

Lobster

Seahorse

Mudskipper

Marine Iguana

Dugong

Shore Birds

Seaweed

■ Shoreline Gang

* Large red, green and brown algae, a different class of plant
* The biggest seaweed – kelp – forms vast underwater forests
* As a source of iodine, seaweed keeps many illnesses at bay

We may be your typical marine vegetation, but there's nothing common or garden about us! Although some of us are classed as plants, most of us strive to be different.

Yes, we have bits that look like leaves, stems and roots, and *like* many plants we use our flat areas to get energy from the Sun via photosynthesis. But *unlike* most plants, we take in nutrients directly from water through our skin – our roots just help us hang on to rocks. Some of us are leathery toughies – gnarly, because we have to endure hours out of the sea, crackling in the blistering Sun. Others have gas-filled bags to keep them afloat (they're a buoyant bunch). In search of sunlight, we anchor almost anywhere. Unlike you, we prefer to sunbathe on rocky shores to sandy beaches – hey, we all need something solid to cling to!

● Largest seaweed: giant kelp (fronds up to 60 m long)
● Growth spurts: giant kelp (up to 50 cm per day)
● Popular uses: sushi, salad, soup, laverbread and agar jelly

Seaweed

Seashells

■ Shoreline Gang

✳ A huge range of animals that fall into three main groups
✳ None of these little critters has a skeleton
✳ They make a protective shell in one or two pieces

You may call us stay-at-homes, but we're sensible types who like a bit of insurance. Just to make sure, we protect our soft bodies within the confines of a hard shell.

We're a diverse bunch that includes brachiopods (lamp shells), bivalves (clams, mussels) and gastropods (snails). Walk along any shoreline, and just beneath the waves or in sparkling rock pools you'll see clinging limpets, grazing periwinkles, jet-propelled scallops, oysters nursing precious pearls, creeping snails and all manner of clams, cockles and mussels. Brachiopods and bivalves live attached to rocks or buried in sand, and feed by filtering out food particles from the salty water. Meanwhile, gastropods prefer to graze on algae on rocks or hunt down their prey as they go about their own whelking business.

● Largest clam: giant clam (up to 140 cm long)
● Boring speed of a shipworm: 15 cm of wood in under a year
● Chemical formula of shell: $CaCO_3$ (calcium carbonate)

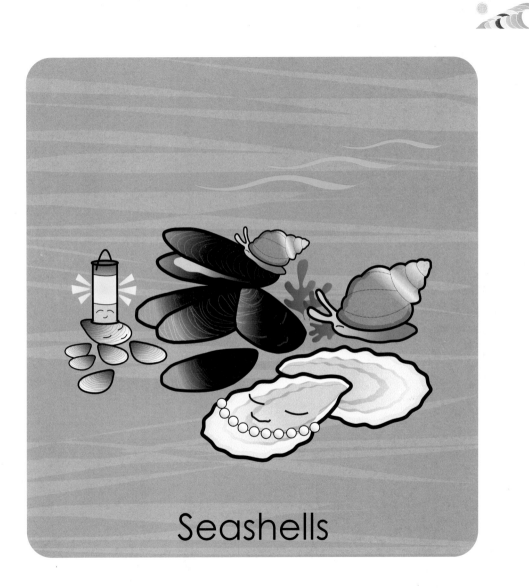

Seashells

Sea Slug
■ Shoreline Gang

* A relative of the sea snail with no shell or internal skeleton
* One of several species of fussy eaters with restricted diets
* Largest and most diverse forms found in warm, shallow waters

Dressed to impress, I rock with the wildest patterns and colours – the more mind-bending the better. You dig me? A hard shell is just a hassle for me – it cramps my style – so I shrug it off when I become an adult.

I cruise the sea floor, using my tentacles to touch, taste and sniff out my prey. I'm something of a specialist in the food department. Collectively sea slugs eat anything – spiky sponges, stinging hydroids and squidgy sea squirts – but each species favours the same one or two of these delights, day in, day out. I particularly like sea anemones. Their stinging cells pass through my gut wall and I pop them out of my back for instant protection. Well, when you're as easy-to-spot and as vulnerable as I am, you've got to be clever to avoid becoming someone else's lunch.

● Scientific name: Nudibranchia
● Adult size: from 20 mm to 60 cm in length
● Distribution: all oceans/worldwide

Sea Slug

Sea Anemone

■ Shoreline Gang

✷ This colourful polyp looks pretty… but is actually pretty nasty!
✷ A small invertebrate that can split itself in two
✷ Stays fixed in one spot, but can shuffle away if it needs to

Hello petal! I'm called a "sea flower" but you don't want to go sniffing me! My gently swaying tentacles are armed with stinging cells that stab with tiny toxic threads. My poison paralyses small fish and prawns, which I pull inside to digest. I'm not a threat to all marine life, though. Clownfish are immune to my toxin and some crabs happily carry me about on their backs.

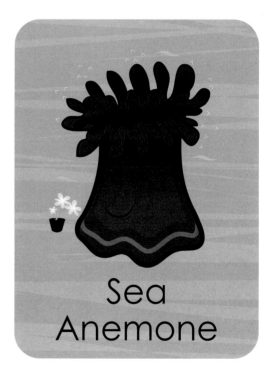

Sea
Anemone

● Scientific name: Actiniaria
● Size: ranges from less than 1.25 cm to nearly 1.5 m wide
● Distribution: coastal waters worldwide, shallow waters and deep oceans

Sea Urchin
Shoreline Gang

* This spiky sea creature has a simple internal shell called a test
* Related to five-pointed starfish, brittle stars and sand dollars
* *Urchin* comes from the Middle English word for a hedgehog

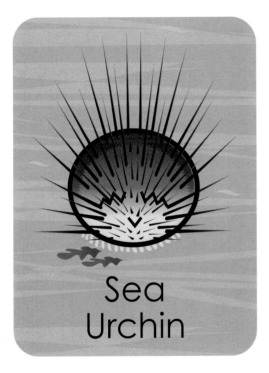

Sea
Urchin

I'm a bristling spiky ball with see-through "tube feet". I pick my way across rock pools and reefs looking for seaweed, algae, sponges and even tough barnacles to scrape off and munch on. Beneath my defensive spines and hard armour plates, I'm a star-shaped softie. Looking at me, you'd never guess I was a tasty treat, but sea otters, wolf eels and humans go mad for my soft centre.

● Typical size range: from 3 to 12 cm wide
● Largest sea urchin: *Sperosoma giganteum* (32 cm wide on average)
● Longest spines: up to 30 cm long (long-spined sea urchin)

Prawn

■ Shoreline Gang

☀ Ten-legged crustacean, related to crab, crayfish and lobster
☀ Hangs around rocky areas, close to the ocean floor
☀ A.k.a. the "insect of the sea"

You'd think I'd be ready for anything: I've got tactile antennae up front; I've got five pairs of legs, some with claws; I even wear a helmet on my head, complete with jagged spear. Yet I twitch and flitter like a nervous wreck. You see, I'm tasty! And while I feed quite peacefully on detritus – not a threat to a soul – my predators often force me to skitter under rocks.

Prawn

● Scientific name: Decapoda
● Largest prawn: black tiger prawn (up to 36 cm)
● Human consumption of tiger prawns: 900,000 tonnes per year

Barnacle

Shoreline Gang ■

- ☀ Tough-nut cousin of the crab posing as a seashell
- ☀ "Winking eyes" that hold tightly to rocks, boats and whales
- ☀ Has both male and female sex organs (hermaphrodite)

Barnacle

With a trick stolen from the Seashells, I've covered my soft body in a hard shell. I cling to rocks and my thick top plates clamp shut to lock out predators and stop me drying out in the Sun at low tide. It's a smart system that allows me to live in inhospitable shore zones, where waves are rough. At high tide I slide my hatches open and stick out my feathery legs to filter food from the water.

- ● Size: 0.5 to 5 cm wide
- ● Number of known species: over 1000
- ● Lifespan: 5 to 10 years

Crab

■ Shoreline Gang

- ✳ Sideways scuttler with ten legs and armour plating
- ✳ Communicates by drumming or waving its pincers
- ✳ Related to lobsters but true crabs tuck their tails under

Klickety klack! I'm a hard-nut shoreline scavenger, winkling food out with my snappy claws. There's very little I won't eat. My favourite place is a rocky seashore, where you'll see me scarpering along the water's edge, eyes (quite literally) on stalks. I'm aware that I'm a tasty fellow, so sometimes I'll carry Sea Anemone on my back for protection. There's a sting in my tale!

Crab

- ● Smallest crab: male pea crab (up to 4 mm wide)
- ● Largest crab: Japanese spider crab (3 to 4 m leg span)
- ● Distribution: worldwide/all oceans

Lobster

Shoreline Gang

* ✳ Crustacean with five pairs of legs, the front three with claws
* ✳ An omnivore who mopes about quietly on the sea floor
* ✳ A tasty critter, protected by restrictions on size when caught

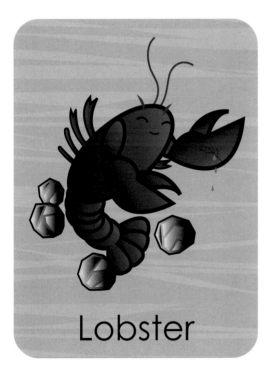

Lobster

Unlike hyperactive Crab, I simply can't be doing with scuttling above the waves. You see, I'm – well – *more upmarket*! Blue blood runs in my veins, thanks to its high copper content. I lead a solitary life, under rocks and in crevices. You might see me marching in (a straight, not sideways) line to egg-laying grounds. If I need to escape, I do it backwards, with brisk jerks of my abdomen.

- ● Heaviest lobster: American lobster (up to 20.15 kg)
- ● Swimming speed: up to 5 m/s
- ● Distribution: worldwide/all oceans

Seahorse

■ Shoreline Gang

☀ Pipefish family member who likes to mate under a full Moon
☀ Wears a crown that is as individual as a fingerprint
☀ The Greek god Poseidon is often depicted riding a seahorse

I'm a funny fish. With my long face, potbelly and head sunk deep in thought, I look like a tiny underwater professor. And I'm not one for galloping about either!

In fact, I'm one of the world's slowest swimmers, wrapping my curly tail around a plant when I need to rest. I'm the only fish that swims bolt upright, flitting through fronds of sea meadows and forests, chasing weeny shrimp, baby fish and plankton. Instead of fishy scales, I have a thin skin that changes colour to blend in with wherever I am. Mating for me is a real performance – I dance with my partner, linking tails and twirling around. When the time is right, I show her the empty egg pouch on my belly and she drops her eggs into it. I'm the only male animal in the whole world that becomes pregnant!

● Size: ranges from 15 mm (pygmy seahorse) to 30 cm (Pacific seahorse)
● Strangest seahorse: leafy sea dragon, with its leaflike camouflage
● Distribution: shallow tropical and temperate waters

Seahorse

Mudskipper

■ Shoreline Gang

* ☀ Amphibious fish that breathes through its skin out of water
* ☀ Can use its strong fins to skip up to 60 cm in the air
* ☀ Escapes predators by resting on tree roots above water

Well whadayaknow? Meet Johnny Jumper, a real fish out of water! With bulging eyes and a frill down my back, you might mistake me for a frog or lizard. I'm right at home when the tide goes out. No scurrying to rock pools or seaweed for me. No, I'm happy in my mud hole. I skip about using super-pumped-up pectoral fins. With bubbly water in my gills, I'm never out of breath.

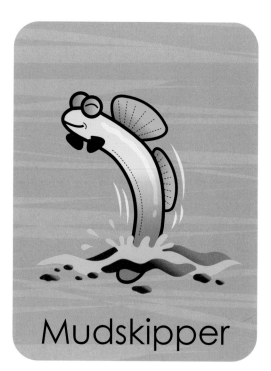

Mudskipper

* ● Average size: 9.5 cm long
* ● Best-known species: *Periophthalmus argentilineatus*
* ● Distribution: tropical mudflats and mangrove swamps

Marine Iguana
Shoreline Gang

* The world's only ocean-going lizard
* A gentle herbivore with a mohawk of spines
* Called the "imp of darkness" by the naturalist Charles Darwin

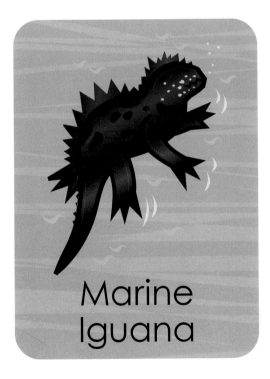

Marine
Iguana

My razor-sharp teeth and long claws give me a fierce look, but I'm no devil. I like nothing more than a juicy nibble on seaweed and underwater algae. My stubby snout lets me get up close to rocks to crop that tricky-to-get-at-but-darn-tasty sea veg, and my horny face is laced with a white salt crust. Hey, when you take in this much salt, why not sneeze some out all over yourself?

* Average size: 0.6 m long (female); 1.3 m long (male)
* Maximum diving depth: 10 m
* Coloration: grey-black with males developing red patches in the mating season

Dugong
■ Shoreline Gang

✳ A large marine mammal also known as a "sea cow"
✳ Related to manatees and elephants
✳ This gentle giant of coastal waters is becoming extinct

They say that sailors used to mistake me for a mermaid. Ha! They must have been at sea too long! I may have lovely smooth brown skin, but I've also got floppy dog jowls and a downturned mouth. I'm no looker!

My real interest is seagrass. Fields of this deliciously juicy plant are found in warm, shallow waters, and I spend my time grazing and cruising between pastures. I love the shallows and often stick my head out of the water for a breath of fresh air. If I need to, I'm able to dive down to 40 metres. Taking deep breaths from the nostrils on the tip of my muzzle, I slip underwater for up to six minutes at a time. Sadly, my meadows are being lost, and I am hunted or snared in fishing nets by mistake. I'm vulnerable to extinction and may soon be gone forever.

● Average size: 2.7 m long
● Oldest dugongs: 70 years old
● Distribution: warm coastal waters from East Africa to Australia

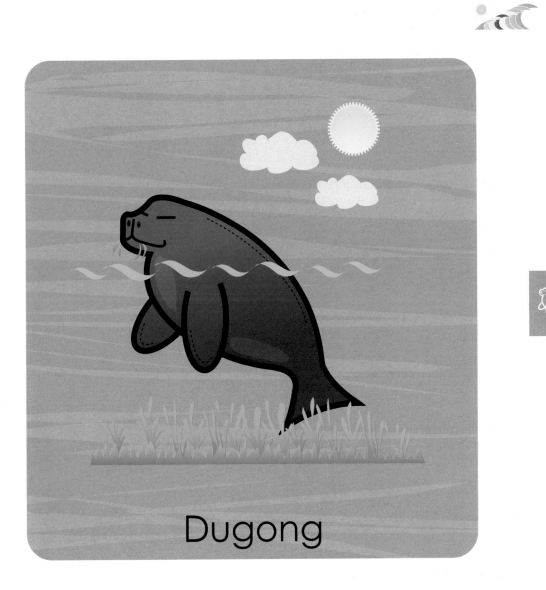

Dugong

Shore Birds

▪ Shoreline Gang

- ✳ Group of wading birds in the intertidal zone
- ✳ Careful and deliberate hunters, some with very long bills
- ✳ Seek out all manner of burrowing invertebrates

We're a bright bunch of beachcombing birds. Strutting along the seashore, sloshing through wet sand and sifting through debris, we work the shoreline in crews.

This is not a life for the fainthearted. It gets pretty chilly, even if you've got a nice down undercoat. The rewards are great – delicious wriggly ragworms, juicy molluscs, sand hoppers and the odd sand-coated mole crab. There's nothing we love better than wading across a good mudflat, where the pickings are rich. Hunting techniques vary: we poke and prod the sand with our bills or do a little stone-flipping. High-tech nerve endings in our bills help some of us detect prey. Different species have different-length bills, which means we can plunder the same coastline without eating another's lunch.

- ● Smallest shorebird: least sandpiper (13 cm tall)
- ● Largest shorebird: Far Eastern curlew (63 cm tall)
- ● Species include: sandpipers, curlews, sheathbills, snipes, plovers, oystercatchers

Shore Birds

Chapter 4
Reef Chillin'

A riot of colour, coral reefs play host to some pretty wild scenes. Life is a carnival, with nearly a quarter of the world's marine species either living on the reef or simply chillin' out down here. The reefs themselves are alive – inhabited by tiny coral polyps – and their towering structures provide a home for a bewildering parade of marine life. The whole reef community depends on the health of lovely Coral – a fragile habitat increasingly endangered by environmental change. Corals prefer warm, sunlit waters, but some hardy types try out the deep, dark and cold northern waters (now *that's* chillin'!).

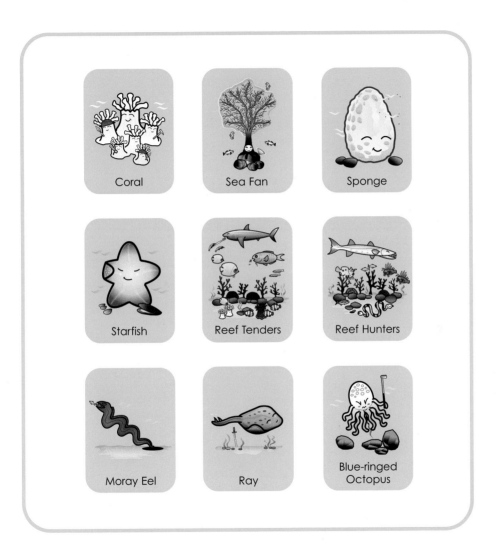

Coral

Sea Fan

Sponge

Starfish

Reef Tenders

Reef Hunters

Moray Eel

Ray

Blue-ringed Octopus

Coral

Reef Chillin'

✳ Soft-bodied house-building animals called polyps
✳ Their hard, stone houses offer protection from predators
✳ Some corals make reefs that can live for thousands of years

We live in high-rise colonies, all crammed in on top of one another. Our white, calcium carbonate apartments might be a squeeze, but there's always plenty of clear, unpolluted water, good light and warmth.

What's known as a "coral head" is actually a vast colony of colourful, genetically identical polyps, each only a few millimetres across. Many hands make light work and there is no shortage of labour here. Most of us build slowly and steadily, but we are master masons. For proof just look at the Great Barrier Reef – you can see it from space! We operate a strict one-polyp, one-house policy with nutrients piped in via a system of canals. We've also teamed up with algae, who take energy from the Sun and provide us with food.

● Coral types: massive, branching, columnar, encrusting and plate
● Deepest-living coral: *Lophelia* (3000 m)
● Largest coral reef: Great Barrier Reef (2600 km long)

Coral

Sea Fan

Reef Chillin'

- ☀ Flexible, non-reef-forming coral rooted to a hard surface
- ☀ This flattened spray of colour is related to the sea anemone
- ☀ Has stinging cells that snare tiny creatures

Fan-tastically elegant and brightly coloured, I am the peacock of the sea. But beware, my flashy whips spell danger for some. Like my cousins Jellyfish, Coral and Sea Anemone, I'm a stinger. (Why else would they call me Gorgonian, after mythical Medusa, who had biting snakes for hair?) Inhospitable you might think, but I provide a safe harbour for tiny goby fish and seahorses.

Sea Fan

- ● Scientific name: Gorgonacea
- ● Number of species: at least 500
- ● Distribution: shallow, tropical waters, especially Caribbean and Indo-Pacific

Sponge
Reef Chillin' ▪

* ✱ Structurally one of the simplest multicellular animals that exists
* ✱ Attaches to hard surfaces and grows into weird shapes
* ✱ Has no stomach, so filters food from the water through pores

Sponge

Chillax dude! I keep things cool by not being overly complicated. What more do you need in life than a body full of holes and channels awash with lovely cold water helped along by microscopic hairs? I use currents to bring me food particles suspended in the water. I also have an awesome superpower – I can regenerate my body if it gets chopped into pieces. Simple pleasures...

* ● Scientific name: Porifera
* ● Number of species: about 5000
* ● Volume of water filtered by a sponge per day: up to 20,000 times its own volume

Starfish

■ Reef Chillin'

✳ Brightly coloured, star-shaped invertebrate echinoderm
✳ A sea-floor dweller with arms called rays and protective spines
✳ Around 2000 species exist, most with five arms

Yup, you guessed it – I'm a total superstar! Devastatingly handsome, I cruise the ocean floor on my tiny tube feet, arms outstretched and on the prowl for tasty tidbits.

A nice mussel, a juicy clam or a delicious poorly fish – anything too sluggish to escape my slow-motion attack has had it. I scramble on top, spit out my stomach and begin digesting straight away. Eating like this means I can gobble things that are bigger than my mouth – it's the ultimate outta-body experience! I may be a no-brainer, but I'm no thickie – I have a complex nervous system with a light-detecting "eyespot" at the end of each arm. And if I lose an arm to a predator I can regrow it. Some species even regrow an entire body from a dismembered arm. Now that's a *star*-quality trick.

● Largest starfish: sunflower starfish (1 m armspan)
● Greatest number of arms: *Labidiaster annulatus* (up to 50)
● Distribution: worldwide/all oceans

Starfish

Reef Tenders

▪ Reef Chillin'

- ✴ An incredibly diverse fish population that inhabits coral reefs
- ✴ These brightly coloured critters bristle with defence strategies
- ✴ Built for manoeuvrability rather than speed

All blinding yellows, deep purples and winks of electric blue, we are a pretty sight indeed. But think again if coral reef spells tropical paradise to you. It's a pitiless world, in which Coral and Sponge battle for territory.

Here on the reef, you need all manner of poisons and spikes just to get you through the day! Parrotfish keeps algae under control when it crunches Coral with its bird-like beak. In swims butterfly fish, its tweezer-like mouth nipping off little coral polyps like grapes. Clownfish seeks protection from predators by hanging out with stinging Sea Anemone. And cleaners wrasse and shrimp run a valet service for sharks and big fish, scrubbing teeth, trimming back dead scales and removing parasites. Nice work if you can get it!

- ● Number of coral reef fish species: 6000 to 8000
- ● Sand produced by parrotfishes crunching coral: up to 90 kg per year
- ● Some parrotfish blow a protective cover of slime around themselves at night

Reef Tenders

Reef Hunters
Reef Chillin'

* Merciless predators who terrorize the reef tenders
* Some, like the whitetip reef shark, hunt in packs at night
* Ambush predators are superhard to spot

Lean, mean and keen to make a killing on the reef, we are one menacing mercenary mob. Among those to fear are tasselled scorpionfish and frogfish, who melt into the undergrowth waiting to ambush unwitting swimmers-by.

Meanwhile, pitiless barracuda patrols the reef edges, its streamlined, torpedo-shaped body allowing for blistering bursts of speed. Blazing out of nowhere, it tears unwary fish into shreds with razor-sharp conical teeth. Bigeye trevally is a diligent hunter who forces smaller fish up against the reef, picking off stragglers in the confusion and panic. Sea snake's flattened tail acts as a paddle for chasing after fish and hunting down eels in their hidey holes. The most flamboyant of our crew is lionfish – a small dude with a "lion's mane" of defensive spines. Ouch!

● Most venomous fish: reef stonefish
● Largest reef predator: grouper – 2.3 m long (Costa Rica, 2010)
● Longest sea snake: up to 2.75 m (yellow sea snake)

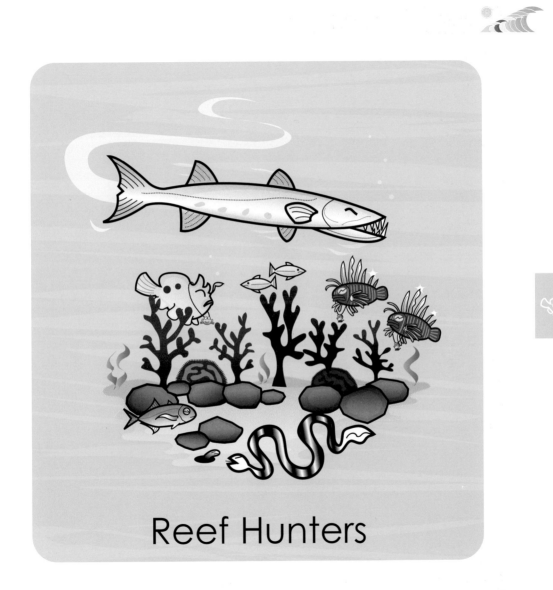

Reef Hunters

Moray Eel
■ Reef Chillin'

✳ Snappy character with a long, wriggly body and smooth skin
✳ A master of camouflage in muddy brown or bright green
✳ Eats fish, molluscs, crustaceans and blue-ringed octopuses

I have a long fin running from tip to tail, a quirky narrow head and a kinda bagginess that makes me look like a sock puppet. But I'm no playtime pal – only big hunters like barracudas or sea snakes will take me on.

I hunt for food at night, but I am also a world-class lurker. Some of my favourite haunts include old pipes and the portholes of sunken ships, where I loiter with my mouth hanging open. Should something tasty pass by, I lunge for it, grasping and biting at it with my razor-sharp teeth. A terrifying second set of jaws in my throat reaches forward to clamp down on prey in my mouth, dragging it into the maw of my stomach. I avoid contact with humans, but I have been known to take a wholesome chunk out of a passing diver – hence my curmudgeonly reputation.

● Smallest moray: Snyder's moray (up to 11.5 cm long)
● Longest moray: slender giant moray (up to 4 m long)
● Distribution: tropical and temperate seas worldwide

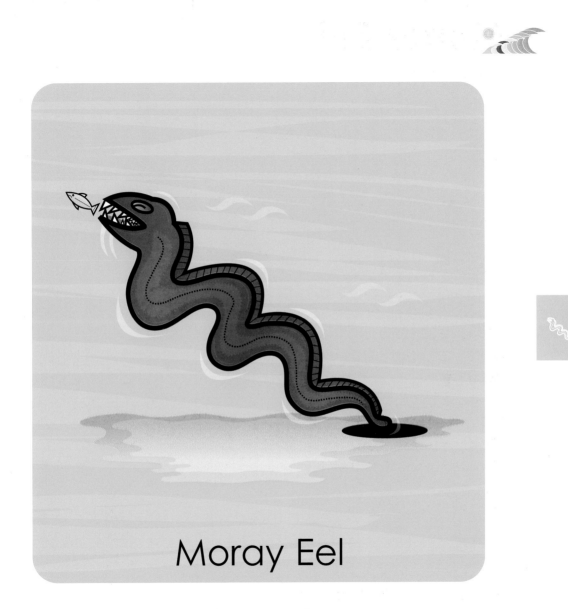

Moray Eel

Ray
■ Reef Chillin'

* ☀ A flat fish with a sting in the tail
* ☀ Grazes the ocean floor, digging out clams and crabs
* ☀ Ray stings are tipped with venom and can be fatal

Hi, I'm Ray, a member of the shark family. I've got stiff, rubbery cartilage rather than hard bones and my rough skin is used on the handles of Japanese samurai swords.

To all and sundry, I am a hooded sorcerer with a rippling, winged cloak and a fearsome reputation. In truth, I've got a gentle nature; I'm docile and curious. I'm more likely to glide up to you rather than hurt you, to see what you're doing... stroking you with a fin. The sting? Always the thing about the sting! Sigh. Yes, some of us (but not all) have a whiplike tail armed with a barbed stinger. More like a tail with a tooth... with venom glands... Nasty, I know, but we all need defence mechanisms. Some of us even give the occasional electric shock, but most of us are happy to cruise peacefully along the seabed.

* ● Scientific name: Batoidea
* ● Largest species: giant manta ray (average 6 m wingspan)
* ● Distribution: coastal warm waters and reefs worldwide

Ray

Blue-ringed Octopus
Reef Chillin'

- ☀ Cephalopod family member, cousin to squid and cuttlefish
- ☀ One of the world's most venomous animals
- ☀ Octopuses have three hearts and blue, copper-rich blood

A dotty killer with enough poison on board to finish off 26 adult humans, I have a beak that can easily slice into a finger. There's no cure for my bite: you could be stone dead within five minutes.

Most octopuses are small – I'm the size of a golf ball with arms. Shy and retiring, I hide away inside empty shells or rock crevices, using my colour-changing camouflage skin to catch crabs, shrimp and small fish unawares. Like all octos, I travel by jet propulsion and when in trouble, I shoot out clouds of distracting dark ink. Provoke me, and my rings flash electric blue in panic, terror and rage. This is when you usually spot me, but by then it's too late!

- ● Average size: 5 cm (body); 10 cm (arms)
- ● World's heaviest octopus: North Pacific giant octopus (up to 71 kg)
- ● Distribution: tidal pools from Japan to south Australia

Blue-ringed Octopus

Chapter 5
Open-water Crew

Over half of the world's surface is open water, far away from the shore and a long way from the sea floor. Most things live in the top 200 m or so, lit by the Sun. They congregate where upwelling currents bring nutrients in from the deep. This is a good place to live, protected from the worst of the Sun's radiation, which can interfere with DNA. There is no fear of drying out, either – temperature extremes that occur on land do not arise here, and creatures are surrounded on all sides by the chemicals and food needed to sustain life. The result is a diverse range of open-water inhabitants. Ready for a dip?

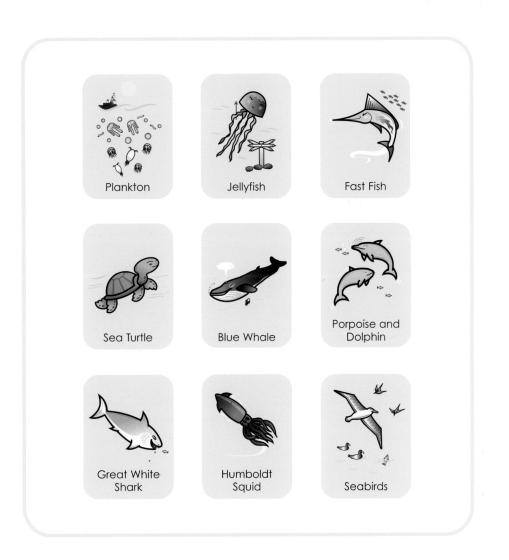

Plankton

Jellyfish

Fast Fish

Sea Turtle

Blue Whale

Porpoise and Dolphin

Great White Shark

Humboldt Squid

Seabirds

Plankton
Open-water Crew

* Microscopic drifters called phytoplankton and zooplankton
* Burst into life in spring, turning parts of the ocean green
* Phytoplankton is the ocean's main source of plant food

Green and serene, we are members of an entire world of microscopic plants and animals that float free in the ocean. All we need for life is light, clean water and food.

Some of us are super-tiny plants known as phytoplankton (say "fye-toe-plank-ton"). Soaking up the Sun's rays, we produce half of the world's oxygen. Floating alongside, gorging on our veggie buffet, are billions of microscopic beasts such as jellyfish, crustaceans, snails, squid and fish larvae. This zooplankton (say "zoo-plank-ton") makes a great snack in itself – it's snaffled by a host of nightmarish creatures who ascend from the deep after sundown. Together we attract forage fish, jellyfish, basking sharks and seabirds, as well as seals, sea lions and whales. You could say we are the ocean's biggest attraction!

* Smallest plankton: picoplankton (0.0002 to 0.02 mm: bacteria, small protists)
* Largest plankton: megaplankton (2 to 20 cm: some seaweed and jellyfish)
* Spring bloom: term for rapid growth of phytoplankton as the oceans warm up

Plankton

Jellyfish
Open-water Crew

* Free-swimming, brainless wonder – the largest kind of plankton
* One of four different classes of related stinging animals
* Some tiny fish hide from predators behind jellyfish tentacles

A jelly-belly dancer, I am a silent and deadly menace of the ocean. I float rather than swim, pulsing softly like a heartbeat, going wherever the ocean currents take me.

I am simplicity itself. I don't have a central nervous system, let alone a brain, and I breathe through my skin, so there's no need for complicated gills. I might be 90 per cent water, but I'm no drip! My trailing tentacles are lined with spring-loaded, venom-tipped spears that fire into the body of anything that happens to get tangled in my tentacles. In some of us, this "curtain of death" is powerful enough to kill a human. Like my photoplankton cousins, I bloom in the right conditions. My microscopic larvae suddenly mature into full-blown jellies, instantly creating a swarm of hundreds of thousands of beautiful blobs.

● Most deadly jellyfish: box jellyfish
● Longest tentacles: lion's mane jellyfish (up to 37 m)
● Distribution: worldwide/all oceans

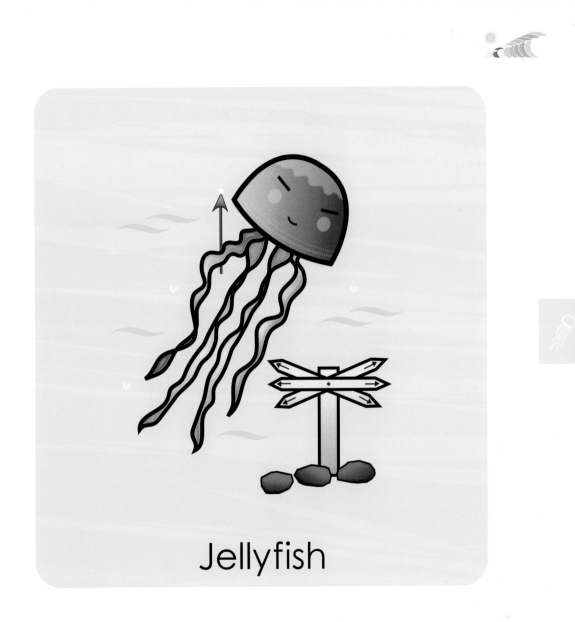

Jellyfish

Fast Fish
Open-water Crew

* Low-friction fish that move like bullets through the water
* Marlin and swordfish swim alone; others, like tuna, form shoals
* These guys do everything on the move – even rest

Ruling the open ocean and built for lightning speed, we are obsessed with streamlining. Just you try to catch a glimpse of us as we flit past with a flash and a twinkle.

We are like sleek torpedoes. Our eyes are flush with our bodies and we have stiff, narrow fins that we can tuck back into hollow slots. Anything that causes drag is out – too many scales, for example. Some of our fastest crew – marlin, sailfish and swordfish – have rapier-like noses that really "slice" through the water! Many of us group together in vast shoals. We love to eat herring and need awesome control to catch them as they swirl in the water. We have a line of extra-sensitive cells running down each side of the body, and this stops us crashing into each other as we give chase.

● Fastest fish: Indo-Pacific sailfish (bursts of 110 km/h)
● Tuna migration: about 10,800 km, from western Atlantic to Mediterranean
● Fastest time taken to cross the Atlantic Ocean: 119 days (bluefin tuna)

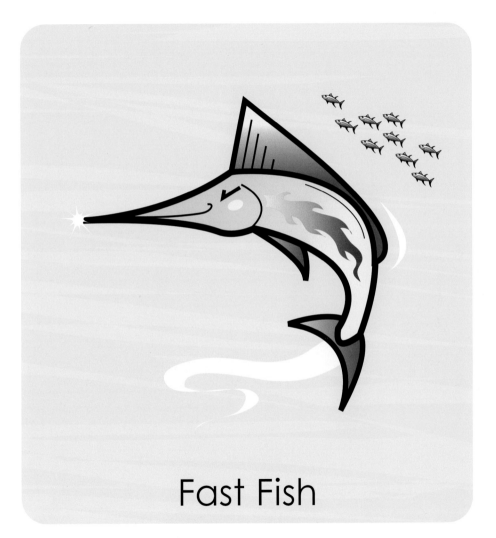

Fast Fish

Sea Turtle
Open-water Crew

✳ Marine reptile, called a chelonian, that can live for 80 years
✳ The only animal on Earth that is immune to box jellyfish stings
✳ Lays eggs by moonlight on beaches

The old lady of the water world, I roam far and wide across the Earth's oceans. I'm a peace-loving soul, sadly on the brink of becoming an endangered species.

I breathe air and have to surface to gulp it down, but I'm much more at home in the water. In fact, I only go ashore to lay my eggs. Life as a youngster is terrifying. Hatching on the beach, I have to make it past beady-eyed seabirds to get to the water. Then I have to dodge hungry fish and predatory sharks. A sharp beak and exceptional night vision allows leatherback turtles to live on a diet of jellyfish, while green turtles are content with seagrass and seaweed, and hawksbills favour sponges. I travel great distances, but I'm cold-blooded so prefer warmish waters – chillier climes just make me sluggish!

● Largest turtle: leatherback (average shell length 200 cm)
● Number of eggs in a clutch: 50 to 200
● Distribution: all oceans apart from the Arctic Ocean

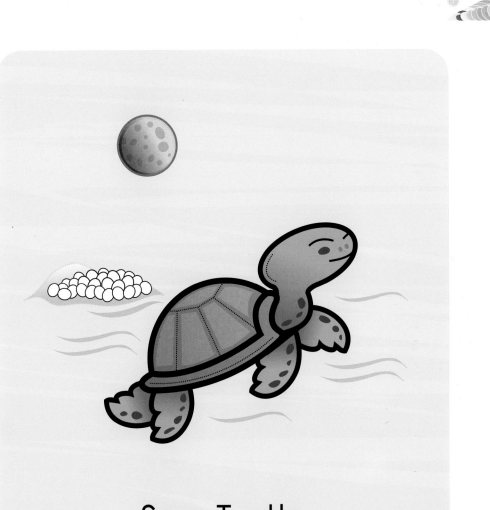

Sea Turtle

Blue Whale
Open-water Crew

* A seagoing mammal, the largest animal ever to have existed
* Can stay underwater for at least 30 minutes and loves singing
* Nearest relative is the land-lubbing hippopotamus

I am the ocean's buried treasure, one of Earth's natural wonders. As big as two schoolbuses and mostly hidden from sight, I am even bigger than the biggest dinosaur!

My heart weighs as much as a car and each eye is the size of a football! When I exhale at the surface after a long dive, my breath condenses and a steamy spray jets 9 m into the air! I'm a hungry fella and it takes more than a couple of servings of krill to fill my huge belly – in fact, I eat up to 6 tonnes every day! I simply open wide and glug. Inrushing seawater pulls in fish and krill, and straining the water out through my big "baleen" moustache leaves them trapped where I can lick 'em off! These truckloads of krill help me build a nice, thick blubber layer to keep me warm. Ain't no barnacles on me... oh yeah, there are!

● Length: up to 30 m
● Average speed: 20 km/h
● Communication: can hear each other over a distance of up to 1,600 km

Blue Whale

Porpoise and Dolphin

Open-water Crew

- Big-brained mammals that live in family groups called pods
- Move by pumping the tail up and down
- There are about 40 species of dolphin and six of porpoise

Meet Porpoise and Dolphin, leaping livewires, the movie stars of the ocean show. You can't miss us – we're a jolly pair, always ready to greet you with a little smile.

Behind Dolphin's shapely bonce and beak is a super-slick brain. No less clever, Porpoise has a smoother profile and shorter snout. We're famed for being smart: we locate fish with sonar clicks and ultrasonic bleeps, and we talk to each other with clicks and whistles as we speed along. We're always learning new tricks – herding fish by blowing bubbles, or hydroplaning on the surface of the water. Speedy Dall's porpoise is the fastest of us all, while spinner dolphin can turn four times in the air. Flipping fantastic!

- Speed of a Dall's porpoise: up to 55 km/h
- Superpod: a group of over 1000 members
- Lifespan: 45 to 50 years (bottlenose dolphin)

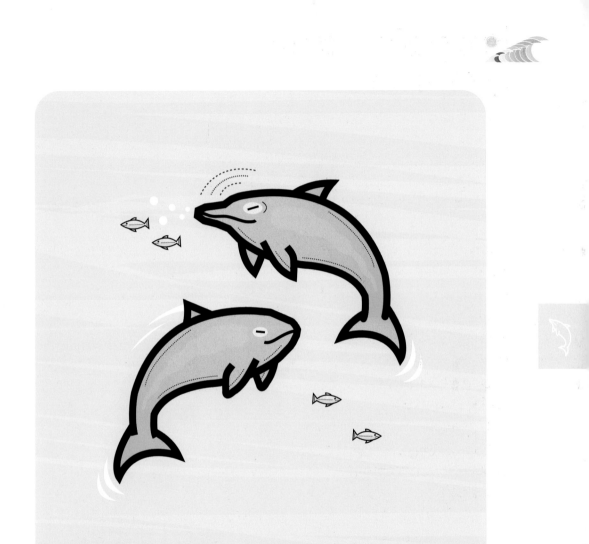

Porpoise and Dolphin

Great White Shark
Open-water Crew

- ✹ The ocean's largest predatory fish
- ✹ Uses its muscle-packed, turbo-charged tail to keep swimming
- ✹ Takes huge bites with jaws that are not attached to the skull

Swift and deadly, I am loaded with sensory equipment and I'm out on the prowl. Oh yeah, mine is a toothy grin other fish really *don't* want to see!

I have detection abilities that put other animals to shame: super-sharp hearing, an acute electrical sense that can make out another fish's heartbeat, and a nose that scents tiny amounts of blood in the water up to 5 km away. My teeth grow in rows that roll forward as old ones fall out, so I have a constant supply of sparkling new teeth! Despite this, most people actually survive a shark attack, because my first chomp is always an exploratory nibble. Humans don't taste good, so I rarely come back for the killer bite. My eyes never close, but boy do I like to roll them back in their sockets when I go in for the kill!

- ● Scientific name: *Carcharodon carcharias*
- ● Largest size: over 6 m long
- ● Number of teeth: up to 300

Great White Shark

Humboldt Squid
Open-water Crew

* This speedy character is smarter than the average fish
* Hides out during the day at depths below 300 m
* Signals to fellow squid by changing colour

I'm a little red devil (so say Peruvian fishermen), riding the Humboldt Current off the west coast of South America. I travel in gangs of a thousand or more, zipping out of the deep and flashing red and white warnings to my pals.

With short fins and a bullet body, I'm not built for comfort, I'm built for speed. My siphon jets me along rapidly, tail first! I may have a touchy-feely side, but my instinct is to eat first, explore later. Two feeding arms bring food back to my mouth, turning it like corn-on-the-cob, while I tear at it with my viciously sharp beak. My gang have even been known to hunt together, "squid-napping" larger animals. If you're diving with me, you need to wear supertough gear: my razor-edged, serrated suckers might not bring the sort of attention you enjoy!

● Largest Humboldt squid: 1.75 m long
● Top speed: over 24 km/h
● Average lifespan: 1 year

Humboldt Squid

Seabirds
Open-water Crew

* Include tubenoses, penguins, boobies, terns and skimmers
* Feed at sea, but nest in vast colonies on land
* This globetrotting gang lives longer than most other birds

Caw blimey! We're a squawking bunch of feathered fine-diners. We'll go to any lengths to get our daily helping of fish, squid and shellfish.

You've got your terns and cormorants, cheeky gulls and frigate birds, skua, guillemots and gannets, pelicans and petrels. Our fishing techniques are diverse – dipping and skimming, dive-bombing and out-and-out underwater pursuit. Waterproofing is a must and we all have an oil gland at the tip of our tail, which we dip into when we preen. There are some real Olympians among us. The albatross has the longest wingspan of all living birds, while the Arctic tern breeds in the Arctic, then flies to the Antarctic over winter and back again. Sadly, the mighty albatrosses are the most threatened birds on Earth.

● Smallest seabird: storm petrel (13 to 26 cm long)
● Albatross wingspan: up to 3.4 m
● Arctic tern migration: about 80,500 km every year

Seabirds

Chapter 6
Deep-down Dandies

This zone and its denizens are shrouded in darkness – it's a place we know less about than the surface of Mars! It's always chilly, even in tropical areas, and the pressure could crush a human skull. A kind of perpetual dandruff of dead plants and animals, called "marine snow", rains down from above. The fish in this bizarre place are small and black with large mouths, stretchy stomachs, no scales and flabby muscles. They are not good swimmers and they're not too pretty, but many can do the most bewitching things with lights – flashing to find or communicate with each other in the dark.

Tripod Fish

■ Deep-down Dandies

☀ Stands on three rays extending from the pelvic fins and tail
☀ Nearly blind, but sensitive to pressure and touch
☀ Has both male and female parts (hermaphrodite)

Cruising slowly, I come to rest above the ocean floor on my very long fin rays. Three spindly supports trail behind me wispily when I swim, but become stiff enough to keep me in position for a feed. Once settled, I turn my face into the current, extending my pectoral fins forwards to "feel" for shrimp and plankton, which I snap up as they drift past.

Tripod Fish

● Scientific name: *Bathypterois grallator*
● Average size: about 30 cm long
● Tripod fish live on the sea floor at depths of up to 5600 m

Anglerfish
Deep-down Dandies ■

* A fishing fish with a glowing "photophore" lure
* Has an upward-pointing mouth and a very flexible jaw
* In some species males attach to, and live off, the females

Anglerfish

Someone once asked me how I came to be called the deep-sea anglerfish. Well, I live in the deep sea, I bait my food... oh, and I'm a fish! I'm not pretty to look at, but my dark, lumpy skin acts as camouflage in the pitch black. I'm rather flabby and a slow swimmer so, like many an angler, I hang about a lot. I simply dangle a glowing lure in front of a mouthful of long, curved teeth, and wait!

● Scientific name: Lophiiformes
● Size: up to 3 cm (male); up to 18 cm (female)
● Nickname: common black devil

Hagfish

■ Deep-down Dandies

☀ Ancient fish, without jaws or real fins
☀ This monster is also called a slime eel
☀ Can turn a 20-litre tub of water into slime in minutes

I am a pirate of the deep-sea floor, swooping in from out of the blackness to attack weak or sick individuals. Fearsome legends surround me – I am known to wriggle into an animal and eat it from the inside out!

I'm quite odious! My primitive "eyespots" only vaguely sense light. I can go for months without eating, so a whole whale carcass rotting on the sea floor is my buried treasure! I have no jaws. Instead, I clamp on with toothy suckers that drag food down my throat. I have a most disgusting habit of producing mucus that reacts with water to produce a thick slime. If I find myself in a tight spot, I loop my body into a knot, which slips down from my head to my tail, ridding me of both my slime coating and my enemy in one *slick* manoeuvre.

● Longest hagfish: up to 127 cm (*Eptatretus goliath*)
● Shortest hagfish: up to 18 cm (*Myxine pequenoi*)
● "Eelskin" wallets, purses and handbags are actually made using hagfish skin

Hagfish

Sea Cucumber

■ Deep-down Dandies

✳ Simple echinoderm, related to starfish and sea urchins
✳ Herds of these invertebrate grazers cross deep-sea mudflats
✳ Makes up over 90 per cent of complex life in the inky ocean

I'm a very simple beast – essentially a squishy bag with leathery skin and a mouth at one end. I am at home on the sea-floor mud plains. These stretch on forever – the largest habitat anywhere on Earth.

The most common creatures down here are the tiny guys that live off the organic debris falling from the ocean above. These tasty wee beasties make up a large part of my diet and I vacuum them up as I plough across the sea floor. My simplicity is astounding – my coral reef cousins can "liquefy" their bodies to pour themselves through cracks, reforming on the other side. I react to danger with gusto, quickly jettisoning my body parts out of my rear. Hard to "stomach", I know, but it certainly distracts my attackers and I can always regrow anything missing.

● Scientific name: Holothuroidea
● Average size: 10 to 30 cm long
● Average lifespan: 5 to 10 years

Sea Cucumber

Hydrothermal Vent

■ Deep-down Dandies

✳ Hot mineral-rich waters gushing out from the sea floor
✳ Forms a chimney called a black or white "smoker"
✳ These fuming funnels are active only for a few decades

Angry, forbidding and surrounded by swirling clouds of particles, I occur where Earth's tectonic plates are moving away from each other.

Seabed rocks are saturated with water. Below them, heat rises from deep inside the planet. It superheats the water circulating in the seabed, forcing it out of cracks to form my tall mineral-rich chimneys. I am home to the only animals on Earth not sustained by energy from the Sun. There are weird blind crabs and shrimp, bright-red giant tubeworms, huge clams and Pompeii worms – Earth's most heat-tolerant complex animal – sitting very comfortably in water as hot as 80 °C or as cool as 20 °C.

● First discovery of a hydrothermal vent: 1977
● Tallest deep-sea vent chimneys: 60 m (Atlantic Ocean)
● Spreading centre: the name for an area where Earth's plates are moving apart

Hydrothermal Vent

Chapter 7
Chilly Chaps

Locked in ice for much of the year, the seas around Earth's poles are parky places. Their chilly inhabitants have to be on their toes to stop freezing their paws, fins and flippers off! That is why this lot are a blubbery crew, with layers of fat beneath the skin to keep them toasty in the cold water. You might think that the going would be too tough in these high latitudes, that animals would go in search of a more comfortable climate, but upwelling waters loaded with vital nutrients and yearly blooms of plankton keep the larders full and the living good. The Chilly Chaps are here to make a splash!

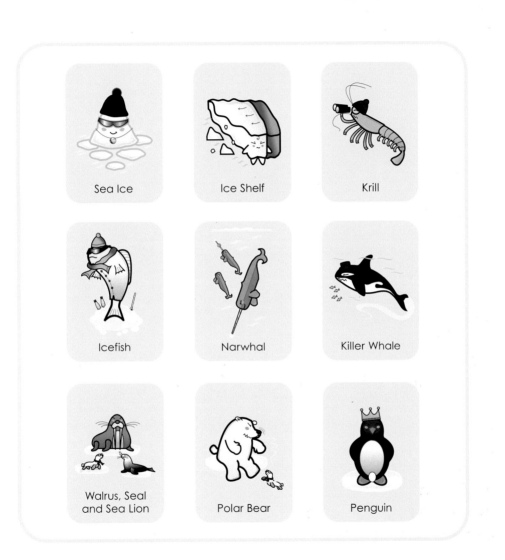

Sea Ice

Ice Shelf

Krill

Icefish

Narwhal

Killer Whale

Walrus, Seal and Sea Lion

Polar Bear

Penguin

Sea Ice

Chilly Chaps

- ❋ Ice that is made when seawater freezes
- ❋ Formed at both poles, it makes up the polar ice packs
- ❋ "Fast ice" sticks to the coastline; "drift ice" floats about

I'm a drifter – I like to go with the *floe*. I appear when it gets cold enough for seawater to freeze. As it does so, it loses some of its salt content. Ice is less dense than liquid water, so I float on top of the sea, changing size with the seasons. I balloon in winter and shrink with the summer melt. With each passing year there's less of me about as the world's oceans heat up. Shame!

Sea Ice

- ● Freezing point of seawater: −1.8 °C
- ● Total area of polar ice pack: 15,600,000 km^2
- ● Thickness of pack ice: 1 to 4 m

Ice Shelf
Chilly Chaps

* Floating platform of ice that juts out into the sea
* Made of compressed snow, the ice is fresh water
* Large pieces of shelf snap off to float free as icebergs

Ice Shelf

I'm totally frigid – a cold shoulder is all you'll get if you nestle up to me. Unlike my bro, Sea Ice, I form on land from snow that gets compressed into glaciers. I slip down to the shore as glacier ice and end up jutting out into the sea like a quiff of frozen water. Being compressed makes my ice denser than normal ice and so almost 90 per cent of me floats beneath the surface. Feel the chill!

● Thickness of sheet: 100 to 1000 m
● Largest existing iceberg: Iceberg B-15; 295 km long, 37 km wide
● An iceberg caused the *Titanic* to sink on her maiden voyage in 1912

Krill
Chilly Chaps

* Shrimp-like crustaceans related to crabs and lobsters
* Like living in swarms of hundreds of millions of animals
* Main food source for a great many sea animals

Life is tough when you're snack food for half the animals in the ocean. We stick together in brain-boggling numbers, keeping a sharp lookout for whales, penguins, squid, seals and many, many fish. Although we swim at just 5 to 10 cm per second, we snap our tails when threatened and fire through the water – we're the ultimate fast food!

We spend our days avoiding predators, shivering in the cold and dark, 100 m below the surface. By night we rise up as a vast cloudy mass to feed on microscopic phytoplankton. We have the largest biomass of any single creature on Earth – more than double that of humans and rivalled only by copepods (mini crustaceans to you). We're tiny but hugely important and without us life in the cold southern seas simply wouldn't survive.

● Scientific name: *Euphasia superba*
● Average size: 5 cm
● Distribution: Southern Ocean

Krill

Icefish

Chilly Chaps

* Group of closely related fish who live in Antarctic waters
* Can cope with temperatures as low as –2 °C
* Has 122 known species to date

Brrr. I'd love to come in from the cold, but I have a mission to undertake in the subzero Southern Ocean: to survive! My cousins and I are specially equipped for the task. Some of us have handy antifreeze proteins in our blood. This prevents our bodies from freezing as we swim. Others have no red blood cells at all, and their thinner blood flows better in these chilly conditions.

Icefish

● Water temperatures that icefish can endure: –2 °C to 4 °C
● Maximum size: 15 cm long
● Maximum lifespan: 15 years

Narwhal

Chilly Chaps

- Medium-sized whale with a single, straight, spiralled tusk (males)
- One of the world's deepest-diving marine mammals
- Travels in pods of up to 20 members

Narwhal

I'm an old sailor of the northern zone, an Arctic wanderer plying ancient routes under the sea ice. I can descend to 1500 m, where I cruise the sea floor hunting for fish, shrimp and squid. My tusk is really an extremely long left incisor tooth. I am hunted by Killer Whale, Polar Bear and Inuit people – my blubber is their main source of vitamin C. Hey, get those guys some oranges!

- Average length: 4 to 6 m
- Tusk length: 2 to 3 m
- Distribution: Arctic waters around Greenland, Canada and parts of Russia

Killer Whale
Chilly Chaps

- A highly intelligent hunter and member of the dolphin family
- A mean predator who travels in troops of ten to 20
- The male dorsal fin can be taller than a fully grown man

I'm a slick-skinned murderer – my strange name, orca, means "from the dead". Any sea creature that sees my tall, black dorsal fin cutting towards it through the water had better say its prayers.

Trust me, I am one merciless beast. I target prey with my fellow henchmen, hunting and harassing them for hours. I'm superswift, snatching whale calves from their mums and drowning them. I terrorize whale sharks and have even suffocated great whites by holding them upside down. By bobbing upright in the water I spot seal cubs sheltering on ice floes. I rock the floating platform or wash water over it to roll them into the water, then I kill them with a tail slap. I'll even surge onto the shore and risk beaching myself to grab tasty sea lion pups. It's a *killer*, I can tell you!

- Average size: 6 to 8 m
- Lifespan: up to 80 years
- Distribution: worldwide/all oceans, but prefer cold water

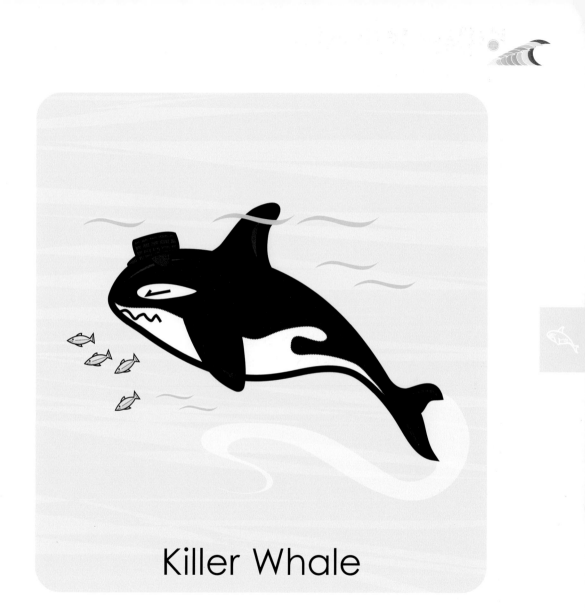

Killer Whale

Walrus, Seal and Sea Lion

Chilly Chaps

* Triplet of fin-footed marine mammals called pinnipeds
* "Honk" to recognize and communicate with each other
* Give birth and raise their young on land

Meet the pinniped family, a bunch of barrel-shaped, blubbery flipper-foots! Weighing over 2000 kg, Walrus is instantly recognizable: think big tusks and moustache.

True seals are sleek-snouted, agile swimmers and boy can we dive. Our hearts beat ten times slower than normal, shutting off the blood supply to non-essential parts. This allows us to stay under water for longer, while a thick layer of insulating blubber keeps us warm. Our cousins, the sea lions and fur seals, are like us but they have more dog-like snouts and tiny ears. Their rear flippers can go back and forth to help them walk on land, while ours are more like a fishy tail – *flippering* useless out of water!

- Scientific names: Odobenidae (walrus), Phocidae (seal), Otariidae (sea lion)
- Largest pinniped: southern elephant seal (up to 4 m long)
- Endangered species: Steller sea lion, Hawaiian monk seal

Walrus, Seal and Sea Lion

Polar Bear
Chilly Chaps

☀ This white North Pole bear measures up to 3 m from tip to tail
☀ Hunts its prey on the sea ice
☀ Mother raises pups in winter, going five months without food

Call me Nanook, my Inuit name – it has a nice ring to it. I'm a real heavyweight – Earth's largest land carnivore. Hang on, what's a land animal doing in this book?

My scientific name, *Ursus maritimus*, should give you a clue. You see, I'm a "maritime bear" – I spend most of my time at sea. Killing every five days, I hunt seals on the pack ice and through the ice floes. I can easily swim 180 km and I'm often spotted over 100 km offshore. I'm really good at conserving heat: my black skin is kept warm by two layers of thick fur. The outer "guard hairs" are transparent, but in bulk look white. I can smell a seal up to 2 km away and I'll wait silently in the water until it surfaces... they always surface. I'll bash through 3 m of snow to get a pup in its lair. It's smashing work!

● Weight of an adult male: up to 800 kg
● Sprinting speed: up to 40 km/h
● Distribution: the Arctic – Alaska, Canada, Russia, Greenland

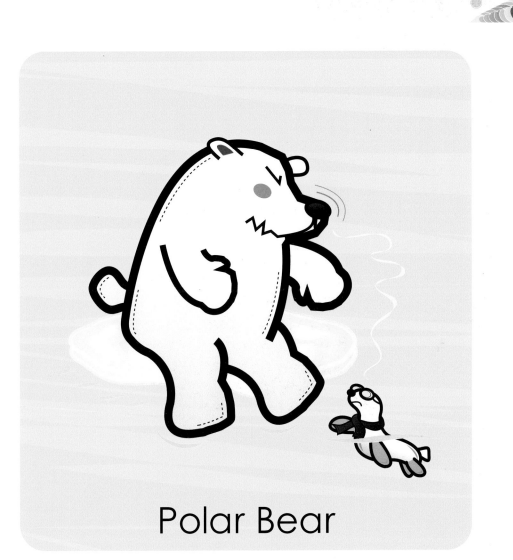

Polar Bear

Penguin
Chilly Chaps

- Chubby Antarctic seabird, fully adapted to life at sea
- Has a streamlined body, flipper wings and heavy bones
- Incredibly powerful and balletic swimmer

I have you fooled! I'm no cute bird in a dinner jacket, but an agile, two-tone ninja. OK, so I get in a bit of a flap out of the water, but what do you expect? I'm squat, I waddle and I can't fly. Get me *in* the water, though, and I'll go expertly in for the *krill*!

I'm a tough old thing, coming in to land on breakers that would snap a ship in two. Fortunately I bounce off the rocks! My dark top/light belly combo makes me hard to spot in the water. Thick, matted feathers and a blubbery layer keep me warm in freezing seas. When it comes to incubating eggs, none do it better than the male Emperor, who balances an egg on his feet for over two months. Hundreds of them huddle together to keep warm in vicious Antarctic storms. That's male bonding for you!

- Largest penguin: Emperor penguin (up to 1.1 m tall)
- Diving speed: 6 to 12 km/h
- Distribution: southern hemisphere (mainly Antarctica)

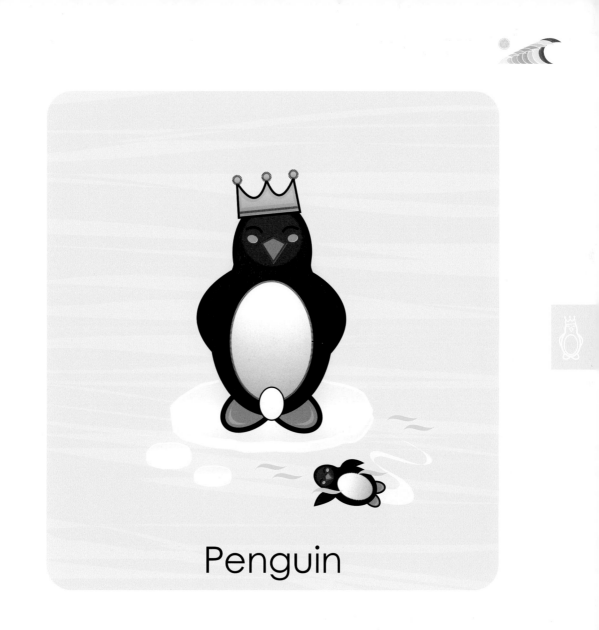

Penguin

Chapter 8
Ocean Explorers

These intrepid explorers demonstrate some of the ways in which humans investigate and exploit the oceans. Life should be a beach for these adventurers – there are still many regions that are largely unexplored – but it seems we humans have a beef with the blue stuff. While 3000 robot probes surface every ten days to beam ocean data back to base, we are whisking food out of the water faster than it can be replaced. Meanwhile, no end of muck floats about, fouling open water and coastlines across the globe. And then there's ocean warming, the greatest threat of all. This could be the time to bail...

Diving

Submersible

Oil Rig

Pollution

Fishing

Diving
Ocean Explorers

☀ The main way to get a glimpse of the underwater world
☀ Specialist equipment allows exploration to greater depths
☀ Used for fishing, research, search and rescue, and pleasure

I'm pure excitement, a portal to a whole new universe. In my simplest form I am one stage up from swimming. But there's more to me than that. Just take a deep breath, dip your head under and you'll find out.

Many people "free dive", which involves holding the breath underwater to fish or for a competition. A snorkel tube and mask make this a bit easier, while wearing flippers gives you additional power. Add an air tank and regulator and you have the scuba-diving kit that frogmen wear. Things get a little more complicated the further down you go, with increasing pressure and decreasing temperatures. And diving is not without its dangers: humans can suffer from deadly, crippling cramps called "the bends" if they surface too quickly from the deep.

● Free-diving record (with fins): 265 m (Dave Mullins, 2010)
● Deepest-diving mammal: up to 3 km (sperm whale, up to 90 mins submerged)
● Average elephant seal dive: up to 1 hour

Diving

Submersible
Ocean Explorers

* Manned or not, this little fella travels down to great depths
* Very sturdily constructed for a life under pressure
* Maintains atmospheric pressure for manned expeditions

Launched off the back of a research vessel, I travel deep into the inky depths. My strong, steel hull can cope with pressures that a human body could never withstand. If I'm not manned I take the form of a robot explorer – a remotely operated vehicle (ROV). Some of my pals have descended to the bottom of the Challenger Deep, the ocean's deepest point.

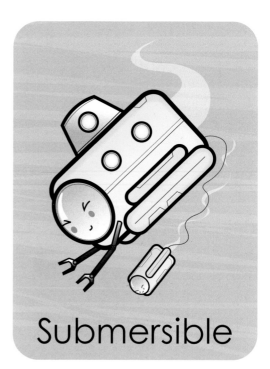

Submersible

● Submersibles that visited Challenger Deep (10,924 m): *Trieste*, *Kaiko* and *Nereus*
● *Alvin*: submersible that discovered the first hydrothermal vent (1977)
● *Argo*: ROV that discovered the *Titanic* (1985)

Oil Rig
Ocean Explorers

* Roughneck who drills for fossil fuels in the sea floor
* This artificial island is also known as an offshore platform
* Ranks among the world's biggest man-made objects

Oil Rig

The ocean bedrock often harbours fossil fuels and gas, and it's my job to extract them. You'll usually find me close to shore, where it is easier to get the job done. Although I'm mostly submerged, I am taller than many skyscrapers. Life aboard me is very risky – drilling and storing flammable substances under pressure means that an outbreak of fire is a constant danger.

- World's deepest-drilling platform: Perdido Spar (2934 m, Gulf of Mexico)
- World's largest platform: Hibernia platform (111 m high, Atlantic Ocean)
- *Deepwater Horizon* oil spill: more than 75 million litres (2010, Gulf of Mexico)

Pollution

Ocean Explorers

- ☀ Litter, industrial waste and sewage – all helping to kill the sea
- ☀ Some are easy to spot (oil spills); others are invisible (sewage)
- ☀ Toxins accumulate and become concentrated in food chains

A dirty, snivelling bunch, we ride the waves as litter, oil spills, industrial waste, shipping waste and raw sewage. Collectively we are messing up the Big Blue, big time!

Litter, our most blatant member, forms unsightly plastic tangles on beaches. In open water, Ocean Current rounds it up into huge "garbage patches". Thick, gloopy oil slicks suffocate all life: zooplankton become deformed, seabirds can't fly, and fish and mammals can't breathe. The real evils are the invisible pollutants. Sewage stifles oxygen by encouraging microbial blooms, while leaks of heavy metals, toxins and nuclear waste from industry can poison wildlife and even end up harming humans who eat polluted seafood. We're a mean bunch and an encounter with any one of us can only end in disaster.

- ● Proportion of litter on beaches that is plastic: 50 %
- ● Number of seabirds killed by plastic waste each year: up to 1 million
- ● Waste thrown into the Mediterranean Sea: 45 million tonnes per year

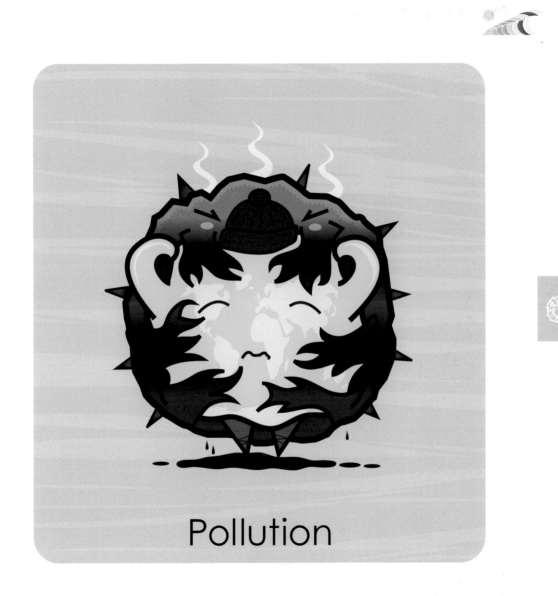

Pollution

Fishing

Ocean Explorers

* Global industry that takes fish from the sea
* Large-mesh nets are used to prevent overfishing
* Turtle-exclusion devices stop the netting of turtles

I have been reaping Ocean's spoils for many thousands of years. For much of this time, the waters were bursting with food that was awesomely good to eat. For each fish pulled out of the sea, more grew to replace them.

Today, better technology and greater demand mean that I now outstrip Ocean's capacity to provide. I have gone high-tech! Thanks to spotter planes, satellite tracking and sonar detection of shoals of fish, fishermen now hit the jackpot every time. But don't be fooled. Cleaning up like this has a price. Even though the mighty cod can live to 20 or 30 years old, few of its kind in the North Atlantic ever get to this age now. Many are caught before they reach maturity, so they never become old enough to spawn and make new fishes. And so the cycle goes on... not!

* Global fish capture: 90 million tonnes per year
* Number of people dependent on fishing: 450 million
* Top five commercial fishing nations: China, Peru, Japan, USA, Chile

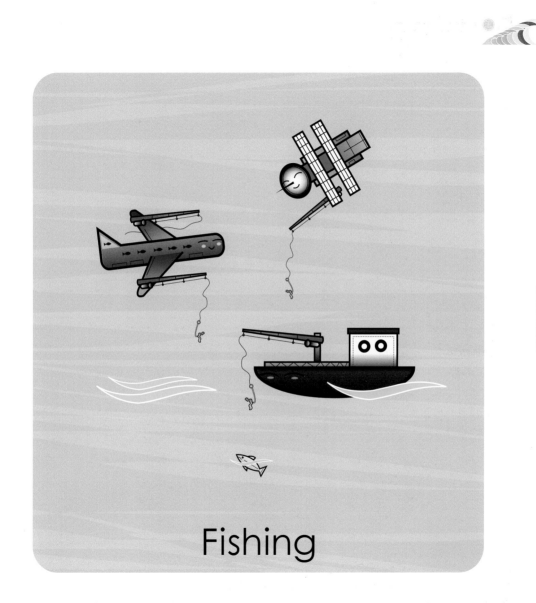

Fishing

Index

Character entries are **bold**

Glossary

Alga (pl. algae) A simple, non-flowering plant, without proper roots, stem or leaves; often single-celled.

Amphibious Describes a creature that can live in and out of water.

Biomass The total mass of animals (or plants) in an area, zone or habitat.

Bivalve A type of mollusc, encased in two hinged shells (e.g. oyster, mussel, clam and scallop), which attaches to rocks with strong, silky threads.

Blubber The layer of insulating fat under the skin of sea mammals and birds.

Brachiopod An invertebrate whose soft body is protected by two hinged shells, which attaches to rocks with a stalk.

Cartilage A tough and flexible connective tissue; some fish have skeletons made from cartilage.

Cephalopod Octopus, squid and cuttlefish; a predatory mollusc with large eyes and tentacles surrounding a beaked mouth; squirts a cloud of inky fluid to confuse its predators.

Chelonian A group of reptiles that includes the turtle family, tortoises and terrapins.

Clutch A group of eggs produced by a reptile.

Colony A community of animals living close together.

Continent Earth's main blocks of land (Africa, Asia, Antarctica, Australia, Europe, North and South America).

Copepod A small crustacean, living as plankton; the most numerous animal on Earth.

Crustacean An invertebrate with a segmented body, jointed legs and a hard outer shell, called an exoskeleton (e.g. crab, lobster, barnacle and copepod).

Cyclone A wind that moves in a circular motion towards an area of low pressure.

Detritus Organic remains, such as bits of dead animals and plants, on which some sea creatures feed.

Echinoderm A marine invertebrate with a hard skeleton, tube feet and a body shape based on a five-pointed star (e.g. starfish, sea urchin and sea cucumber).

Floe A sheet of floating ice.

Gastropod A mollusc with a large, muscular "foot" and a spiral shell (e.g. sea snail and whelk).

Herbivore An animal that feeds only on plants.

Hermaphrodite An animal with both male and female sexual organs.

Hydroid A tiny aquatic invertebrate with a tube body and a ring of stinging tentacles around the mouth.

Invertebrate An animal without a backbone.

Latitude Imaginary lines that divide Earth horizontally – high latitudes are zones near the poles; low latitudes are near the Equator.

Mammal A warm-blooded animal, often with hair, that gives birth to live young.

Glossary

Migration The seasonal journey made by an animal from one region to another.

Mollusc A member of a group of aquatic invertebrates that includes gastropods, cephalopods and bivalves.

Monsoon A wind that changes direction with the seasons.

Multicellular Any lifeform with more than one cell.

Omnivore An animal that eats both plants and other animals.

Photosynthesis The process by which plants and algae use sunlight to turn carbon dioxide and water into food.

Pinniped A group of marine mammals (seals, walruses and sea lions).

Polyp A single member of a coral colony, a hydra or a sea anemone.

Predator Any animal that hunts other animals.

Radiation (Sun's) Energy that comes from the Sun, in the form of infrared waves, visible light and ultraviolet waves.

Saline Describes water that is salty.

Siphon A tube through which sea animals suck things in or blow things out.

Sonar The sound waves used for echolocation (detecting objects underwater).

Tectonic plate A large chunk of Earth's crust that moves as one piece.

Venomous Describes an animal that carries poison, and that can bite or sting.